MOUNTAIN MAN

MOUNTAIN MAN
The Life of Jim Beckwourth

MARIAN T. PLACE

Illustrations by PAUL WILLIAMS

CROWELL-COLLIER PRESS
COLLIER-MACMILLAN LIMITED, LONDON

Library of Congress Catalog Card Number: 79-119129

The Macmillan Company
866 Third Avenue
New York, New York 10022

Collier-Macmillan Canada Ltd., Toronto, Ontario

Printed in the United States of America

FIRST PRINTING

Contents

MOUNTAIN MAN

Introduction

"I was born in Fredericksburg, Virginia, on the 26th of April, 1798. My father's family consisted of thirteen children, seven sons and six daughters."

Thus Jim Beckwourth, son of a white Virginia planter and Negro slave mother, began the story of his exciting life as a fur trapper and Indian trader in the far West. The story was published in 1856 under the title *The Life and Adventures of James P. Beckwourth, Mountaineer, Scout and Pioneer, and Chief of the Crow Nation of Indians*. Jim did not actually write the book because he had never been to school. Instead, he related his experiences to a newspaper man who wrote down what Jim said. The book was widely read over a century ago, and is still very popular today. It brought Jim enduring fame as one of the most colorful individuals in the frontier West.

Nowadays historians call men like Jim Beckwourth and his comrades "mountain men" because they chose to spend their lives trapping for beaver in the Rocky Mountain country. All were men of extraordinary courage and seemed to thrive on hardships and danger. They disliked living in settlements where they were within shouting distance of their neighbors. All possessed an overpowering desire to venture deep into the wilderness. If they were lucky (and many weren't), they survived encounters with grizzly bears, hostile Indians, blizzards, and long bouts of starvation.

Jim knew all the great mountain men—Jed Smith, Jim Bridger, Tom Fitzpatrick, Kit Carson, and a score of others. Although they were white men and he was a Negro, he traveled in their company as an equal. They didn't care an owl's hoot whether a man was tall or short, rich or poor, black or white, educated or illiterate, bathed frequently in icy mountain streams, or smelled worse than a bear's den. Mountain men judged and respected a man for his courage and strength, his coolness in the face of frequent danger, his wit and good nature, and his skill as a trapper or hunter.

Whenever these grizzled frontiersmen lounged about their campfires, they entertained each other by telling tall tales, the more outlandish and spine-chilling the better. In time Jim became an accomplished storyteller. However, his exaggerations were never more than salt on wild meat. The yarns he told were based on actual happenings.

Jim was in his late fifties when he told his story to T. D. Bonner, a newspaperman. In this account which is based on his book, except for very slight editing and a few changes in punctuation, the dialogue will be those very words Jim used in relating his story to Mr. Bonner. Wherever possible the famed mountain man will speak for himself.

1

A Very Young Man Goes West

"When I was but about seven or eight years of age, my father removed to St. Louis, Missouri, taking with him all his family and twenty-two Negroes. He selected a section of land between the forks of the Mississippi and Missouri rivers twelve miles below St. Charles, which is to this day known as Beckwourth's settlement." The whole region, Jim explained, was "a howling wilderness inhabited only by wild beasts and merciless savages."

Unfortunately Jim said nothing more about his family, or his early childhood in Virginia, or the long journey to St. Louis. We can only guess that his father moved west in order to increase his land holdings. The family probably traveled overland with horses and wagons from Virginia to the Mississippi River, and ferried across that broad muddy stream to St. Louis. When they arrived in 1805 or 1806, the state of Missouri had not yet been formed. St. Louis was a tiny outpost in a vast unexplored wilderness known as the Louisiana Territory, which Congress had purchased from France only two years earlier. Through this so-called Louisiana Purchase, the United States acquired 830,000 acres extending from Canada to the Gulf of Mexico, and from the Mississippi westward to the Rocky Mountains. News spread slowly in those days. However, once land-seekers learned thousands of acres of rich farm land now were open to settlement by Americans, they flocked across the Mississippi.

The water lapping the west shore was deep enough so canoes and flatboats could tie up at the bank. When the Beckwourth family stepped ashore, they found themselves in the midst of a small hamlet. Log dwellings had been raised in hit-or-miss fashion over a wide level area extending from the river to the foot of a steep bluff. Many of the three thousand inhabitants were Frenchmen who made their living by hunting and trapping. But there were an increasing number of Americans now, frontiersmen and sunburned farmers, a few shopkeepers and tavern owners, a housewife or two, and a small encampment of friendly Indian families. The streets were little more than meandering footpaths, and the whole area was ridden with flies and fleas.

Regrettably, Jim included no information in his

book describing how the Beckwourth family settled in their new location some twenty-five miles north of St. Louis. We know nothing about how much land was cleared, how many trees felled for buildings and fences, how many acres planted, or how deer, wild turkeys, geese, and fish were obtained for food. Other families were established nearby so the Beckwourths did not feel too isolated. The Indians roundabout seemed to resent the newcomers taking over the land which had been their hunting ground for centuries. But so far they had expressed their anger only in small acts of vandalism, such as tearing down fences or riding their horses back and forth across ripening crops.

At harvest time Mr. Beckwourth asked Jim if he felt man enough to ride to the mill with a sack of corn. Jim nodded eagerly. Being asked to go on an errand all by himself thrilled the youngster. Even though he was only eight or nine years old, he was anxious to prove he could be trusted. His father brought a gentle horse from the pasture, placed the sack of corn across its back, and lifted his son on top. Jim took a firm grip on the reins, banged his bare heels into the horse's flanks, and headed for the mill two miles away.

When he came in sight of a neighbor's house, he slowed the horse to a walk. Usually children were playing in the yard, but today it was deserted. When Jim halloed, no one answered. A little puzzled, he slipped off the horse, wrapped the reins around a fence post, and ran toward the house, calling happily. But his joy turned to horror when he came upon the bodies of the parents and their children strewn about the porch and doorway. All had been scalped.

The next thing Jim remembered was flinging himself into his father's arms and sobbing out the dreadful story. He couldn't remember riding home or what had happened to the corn. His father comforted him and then, Jim said, "immediately gave the alarm throughout the settlement, and a body of men started in pursuit of the savages." In two days the band returned, bringing with them eighteen Indian scalps. As Jim explained, "the backwoodsman fought the savage in Indian style," which meant scalp for scalp.

For months the Beckwourth family and their neighbors lived in dread of another such raid. The men and youths, with guns in hand, stood watch day and night. The following spring Jim tagged along when his father and others gathered on the bank of the Mississippi to spy on a large body of Indians congregating on the opposite shore. They were riding about in full war regalia and brandishing their bows and lances. Obviously they were working themselves into a frenzy that could only lead to an attack on the settlers in the region.

Jim's father and the others talked quietly and

withdrew to their homes. But that night, Jim said, his father and some of his men rode off to St. Louis. They joined a large force, rowed across the river under cover of darkness and attacked the Indian camp. After a fierce fight, the Indians were defeated and fled north. The settlers on both sides of the river remained vigilant until federal troops arrived to protect them. Months later the chiefs signed a peace treaty with government officials. Only then did family life and business resume a normal pace in and around St. Louis.

In those days a boy learned how to farm and hunt from his father and older brothers. Occasionally if there were several sons in a family, one might be apprenticed to learn a trade. Thus when Jim was fourteen, his father took him to St. Louis and apprenticed him to a blacksmith.

"I took to the trade with some unwillingness at first," Jim admitted, "but becoming reconciled to it, I was soon much pleased with my occupation." (Jim probably didn't speak in such a stilted way. The newspaperman to whom Jim told his story "polished" Jim's colorful speech so it would measure up to the literary standards of that time.)

The fact that Jim's father chose him to be an apprentice tells us more than Jim put into words. Jim must have been strong, intelligent, and dependable, or his father would not have favored him in this way. He must have been fond enough of Jim to want him to be more than a field hand. A blacksmith was an important and much respected craftsman. True, an apprentice had to work many years under his master before he could set up his own business. But in the end, he emerged as a skilled worker capable of earning a good living.

Very likely Jim's first task was pumping the bellows to keep the fire hot in the blacksmith's forge. Perhaps he held the horse's head while the blacksmith secured the iron shoes on its hooves. Jim worked from dawn to dusk six days a week. He slept on a pallet at the back of the shop, washed at the horse trough, and took his meals with a Negro family nearby. On Sundays he was free to roam. With other boys his age he explored the forest nearby, swam in the creek, or strolled about the riverfront.

By this time St. Louis had two thousand more people than it had when the Beckwourths arrived. Several hundred of these were Negroes who lived in small cabins at the foot of the bluff. The able-bodied men worked in the warehouses, livery stables, and freighting offices because the port commerce was thriving. Some were slaves but a good portion were freemen. Their wives and daughters worked as servants for the wealthy French and American families whose spacious homes were set amidst park-like estates atop the bluff.

A mile-long levee of crushed rock had been built

to protect the riverbank from being eaten away by the powerful current. The wharves, constructed of stout oak planking, were lined with canoes, flatboats, and seventy-foot-long keelboats. Jim and his friends liked to climb up on a mound of crates and bales and watch while the boats were loaded or unloaded. They were fascinated by the French-Canadian boatmen who poled and towed the keelboats up and down the river. These men sang a lot and wore colored sashes about their waists and red feathers in their caps.

However, the individuals whom the boys watched with the greatest excitement were the trappers newly returned from the Rocky Mountains. From the moment these sunburned bearded men set foot on the wharves, they were surrounded with young admirers. The boys clamored for stories about buffalo hunts, Indian attacks, and hair-raising encounters with grizzlies. They shuddered when they saw one badly scarred man who had been bitten and clawed by a grizzly bear and lived to tell about it. Usually the trappers made a beeline for the nearest taverns. But afterwards some would saunter outside and reward the boys with tales that soon had them wide-eyed and quivering with excitement. Sometimes

Jim's first task as a blacksmith's apprentice was pumping the bellows.

the trappers let them handle a warrior's scalp, or a war shield, or a necklace fashioned from a bear's claws.

Jim must have been spellbound by these tales because gradually he became more and more dissatisfied with learning his trade. Even if St. Louis was a lively place, it seemed that the real excitement was taking place a thousand miles or more up in the mountains. In contrast, a blacksmith's life was terribly dull! But because he wanted to please his father, Jim stayed with his apprenticeship until he had finished the training. By that time he couldn't bear to work another hour in a shop. He went home and told his father that he was a grown man now, past twenty-one and wanted to see "the great western wilderness."

At first his father tried to persuade him to return to his trade. But then he relented and gave Jim a horse and saddle and a little money. And, as Jim said, "He bade me God speed upon my journey."

2

"Ho! For the Mountains"

Jim sped back to St. Louis. On arriving he tied his horse to a hitching rack and washed his face and hands in a watering trough. He wanted to look his best when he inquired about a job. After he shook the dust from his jacket and combed his dark wavy hair, he threw back his shoulders and stepped out along the board sidewalk. He walked as a free man would walk with a firm swinging stride. During the years of his apprenticeship, his shoulders had broadened and his arms bulged with hard muscles. Jim had inherited his father's facial features and light skin, and his mother's dark eyes. He knew he was good-looking because more than one pretty girl had told him so. Underneath his wool trousers and dark flannel shirt, he wore a canvas belt next to his skin.

In it was hidden the money his father had given him, along with a slip of paper stating that James Beckwourth was a free man and the rightful owner of a brown mare and saddle.

Brimming with confidence, Jim stepped into an office in the warehouse headquarters of the Rocky Mountain Fur Company. Soon he found himself talking to General William H. Ashley, who owned the firm in partnership with Andrew Henry. Jim knew both men by sight and reputation. Ashley was lieutenant governor of the newly formed state of Missouri and a brigadier general of the state militia. He was the business manager of the company. Andrew Henry was a well-educated gentleman, equally skilled in playing a violin or shooting a rifle. Since he was experienced in managing trappers' brigades and trading posts, he was in charge of the firm's operations in the mountains.

The year before, Ashley and Henry had hired nearly one hundred single young men to ascend the Missouri River to its headwaters in the Rocky Mountains (in present-day Montana) and trap for beaver. Unfortunately, during their first year of operation, the partners suffered several disasters. Indians killed over twenty of their men, and one of their keelboats transporting $10,000 worth of supplies and trade goods up the Missouri sank in water too deep and swift to permit salvaging any of the cargo. But in spite of these reverses, the partners planned to send a second expedition to the mountains. They were willing to run the risk of further disasters because the profits from trapping were so great. Beaver pelts were in tremendous demand in the United States and Europe due to a fashion craze for wide-brimmed hats made of the dense, rich pelts. No gentleman or lady of means would sally forth without one. Since Rocky Mountain beaver skins had a thick, velvet-like texture, they brought premium prices when sold at the raw-fur market in St. Louis. Thus, if the partners had even one good year in business, both would become wealthy.

Naturally, when Jim inquired for a job, the first thing General Ashley asked him was whether he was an experienced trapper. Jim shook his head and answered that he had just completed his apprenticeship as a blacksmith.

The general smiled broadly and hired Jim right then and there. Then he explained why the firm needed a blacksmith. Rather than expose his trappers to more Indian raids and risk losing another cargo in the river, the general planned to move his new expedition overland. He would avoid the upper Missouri and Yellowstone country and dispatch the men throughout the Bighorn and Absaroka mountains in present-day Wyoming.

No other fur company had attempted to travel that far overland because supposedly there was no way a supply train could cross range after range of mountains. However, meantime one of the firm's trapping parties led by Tom Fitzpatrick and Jed Smith had discovered a broad low pass over which horses and even wagons could pass. This was South Pass, which would be much used two decades later by covered wagons traveling to California and Oregon. Fitzpatrick and Smith had learned about the pass from the friendly Crow Indians and traveled over it to trap beaver in the many creeks and rivers which flowed from the western slope of the Rocky Mountains into the Colorado, Snake and Columbia rivers.

General Ashley told Jim that he expected to buy enough horses so his men could ride horseback and transport supplies and trade goods on pack mules. Having a blacksmith along could spell the difference between the success or failure of the party in reaching the mountains. If the animals became sore-footed for lack of shoes and could not walk, the entire operation would have to be abandoned. However, the general added, Jim would have to report to work the next morning because the departure date was only two days off.

Jim assured General Ashley that he could start work at once. He was eager to be on his way to the mountains. He had liked the general at first sight even though he seemed a trifle old to be traipsing about wilderness country. The general was at least forty years old and rather small and slight. Yet he gave the impression of being a man with plenty of backbone and vitality. So when the general offered his hand to seal their agreement, Jim clasped it firmly. The general then wrote Jim's name in the roster of employees and had Jim place his mark, an '*X*', beside it. After receiving a few instructions, Jim left the office.

Jim was grateful for the money his father had given him because he was able to outfit himself properly. He bought heavy wool underwear and socks, a winter jacket and cap, a towel and bar of soap, and other articles which he packed in a small canvas sack. He also added two blankets and a ground cloth for protection against dampness and rain. He rolled these tightly and fastened them behind his saddle. That evening he celebrated his going away with friends.

The next morning Jim rode to the camp on the outskirts of St. Louis where General Ashley was overseeing final preparations for the expedition's departure. After he picketed his horse and reported to the general, he got right to work. A portable forge had been set up, and a young lad already had a fire going. Jim shoed several horses and checked the hooves and gear of every other animal. During the long years of his apprenticeship, he had gained a wealth of knowledge about horses. He could tell almost at a glance an animal's good and bad points. He was relieved to see that the general had purchased good stock and equipment. This improved their chances of going all the way to the mountains. Jim worked steadily throughout the day, with little more than glances at the other men. Most appeared to be about his age, but none took time to talk. Each minded his own business and strove to make a good impression on the general.

When the cook shouted that supper was ready, everyone whistled and rushed to line up behind General Ashley. From a box which served as a table, he picked up a tin plate and served himself beef stew, boiled potatoes and carrots, and biscuits. Next he dolloped the meat with bottled peppersass, poured syrup over the biscuits, and accepted a mug of coffee from the cook. Then he walked over to a crackling bonfire and sat crosslegged on the ground. The crisp October air made a campfire a necessity after sundown. Moments later the general's clerk joined him, and an older man clad in a buckskin suit and moccasins. This was Moses Harris. According to camp gossip, Harris was ill-tempered and contemptuous of greenhorns. Still, he was a good man to have along. He was a fine hunter and had spent many seasons with the Indians who roamed the Platte River from its headwaters in the mountains to its confluence with the Missouri.

After the men had eaten to the bursting point, they lounged about the fire. Jim counted twenty-nine all together, including himself. Later the general rose and made a short speech. He explained that because a journey to the mountains was a hazardous undertaking, the safety and well-being of everyone depended on working together. Every man except himself and Harris must take his turn at night guard duty. Each was to do his share of hauling water and gathering firewood. Anyone who started a fight would be thrown out of camp and forced to make his way alone back to St. Louis.

The men murmured their assent and soon after began laying out their blankets. Jim spread his ground cloth first, and laid his blankets along one-half its width. He took off his boots, put them at the head and covered them with his hat. Then he crawled fully clothed between the blankets and tucked the remaining half of the ground cloth about him. Moments later he was asleep.

The next morning the cook banged on a kettle with an iron spoon to rouse the men. After a hearty breakfast Jim helped load packs on the mules. Then he saddled his horse and waited for the general to give the signal to move out. At long last Ashley stood in his stirrups, waved his hat, and shouted, "Ho! for the mountains!"

Jim and his companions waved their hats and shouted at the top of their lungs. Then they chirked to their horses and fell into line, riding two and three abreast behind Ashley and Harris, with the mule train bringing up the rear.

3

A Dangerous Winter Journey

"We started on the 11th of October [1823] with horses and pack mules," Jim related in his book.

For four weeks Moses Harris led the Ashley expedition along a well-worn wagon road which followed the Missouri River westward. The company never was out of sight of small farms and passed an occasional sawmill and riverfront trading post. Since the forest bordering the trail abounded with deer and wild turkeys, and the sloughs were noisy with geese and ducks, the men ate their fill morning and night of meat, biscuits, and gravy.

Jim liked his new life—the traveling through new country, living outdoors, even night guard duty. After the first few days the men got to know each other better and the general, too. Soon they were joshing back and forth and sharing chores. To Jim the journey was one long, happy picnic.

About mid-November the company reached the point where the Missouri River turned abruptly to the north. Since there were no trading posts beyond, the general restocked his food supplies at a post run by men named Ely and Curtis. Meanwhile Jim examined every horse and mule and informed Ashley that they could not possibly make it to the mountains without the addition of another fifty horses. The general had not purchased enough extra mounts to replace those that turned up lame in spite of Jim's constant care.

This posed a real problem. There were no horses to be bought in the sparsely settled region. It would take too long to send men back to St. Louis for more. Although there was a village of Kansa Indians close by, Ely and Curtis reported the few bony ponies they possessed wouldn't even make good crow bait. The best horses, they added, were available from the Pawnee Indians who ranged the Republican River valley. However, the Republican was three hundred miles to the north, in present Nebraska. Traveling out across the prairie to reach it was exceedingly hazardous during the winter months.

When General Ashley told Moses Harris this, the scout promptly volunteered to search for the Pawnee encampment. The general accepted the offer and that night asked for a volunteer to accompany Harris on the risky venture.

Not one single man spoke out. This was not because of the long distance or hazards of a winter journey, nor because of the scout's dour disposition. They were reluctant to volunteer because Harris had a reputation for having a "great leg." That is, he could travel exceedingly long distances and endure hardships that killed lesser men. And, as Jim said, "It was whispered that whoever gave out on an expedition with Harris received no help from him, but was abandoned to his fate in the wilderness."

When an embarrassing silence developed, General Ashley looked sternly from one man to another. Still no one spoke out. Finally, the general fixed his glance on Jim and asked him to go, because Jim would be sure to select the horses best suited to the company's needs.

Jim said, "Being young, and feeling ambitious to distinguish myself in some important trust, I asked leave to have a word with Harris before I decided."

Since the general was willing, Jim and the scout stepped aside to talk. Harris scrutinized Jim closely and then remarked patronizingly, "Do you think you can stand it?"

"I don't know," Jim replied slowly, "but I am going to try. But I wish you to bear one thing in mind. If I should give out on the road, and you leave me to perish, if I have strength to raise and cock my rifle, I shall certainly bring you to a halt!"

Harris answered grumpily, "It will be your own fault if you tire out."

The next morning each filled a canvas bag with twenty-five pounds of flour, sugar, coffee, and bread. They tied a coffee pot, skillet, and two blankets apiece on their saddles. The general gave each a good rifle and ample ammunition for hunting. That first day they rode thirty miles. Since Jim was now hardened to riding long distances, he was not overly tired when Harris stopped to camp alongside a creek. Jim started the fire and made camp while Harris shot two fat turkeys from a tree nearby. After a hearty meal eaten in silence, the two picketed their horses securely and rolled in their blankets.

When they wakened in the morning, their horses were gone. Judging from the fresh moccasin tracks visible on the heavily frosted ground, the horses had been stolen by Indians. Harris not only was furious. He refused to return and face Ashley and suffer the taunts of the other men. To save face he declared that he was going to continue on foot to the Pawnee camp. Jim could do as he dang well pleased.

Although Jim was not afraid to face the general, he grimly determined to prove to Harris that he was no weakling. So he readily agreed to stick with the scout. Each shouldered his pack and blankets and trudged on. According to Jim they marched over forty miles the first day before Harris gave in. Even though Jim was so tired that he ached from head to foot, he was proud that he had shown Harris he had a "great leg" too.

On the third day they left behind the sheltering groves of the broad Missouri River watershed and moved out across endlessly rolling hillocks covered with knee-high prairie grass. At times the sky darkened with the passing flights of thousands of waterfowl. For the next few days they averaged about thirty miles daily. Numbing cold, a pounding north wind and frequent snow squalls slowed their pace, as did the shortening hours of daylight. But at long last they came onto a muddy meandering river which Harris said was the Republican.

The Republican had been named years before by French trappers. When they came to a stream, they might find no Indian who could tell them the name, or they might meet more than one tribe of Indians, each of which had a different name for the stream. One historian thinks the French trappers gave this river its name, *républicain* in French, possibly because the Indians they met along its banks chose their chiefs from among their people, instead of having the post hereditary and passing from father to son. But this is only a guess.

Much as Jim was thrilled to have reached the Republican, he was far more interested in finding the Pawnee village. Much to both men's dismay, there was none to be seen in any direction. They walked miles upstream and down, and they even explored the course of a tributary creek but saw no living soul. There were plenty of blackened fire pits and piles of refuse to indicate that the Pawnees had camped in the region. By this time, Jim said, Harris was very glum. He guessed the Indians had moved to their winter campsite along the more sheltered banks of the Loup River, many miles to the northeast. So if he and Jim were to obtain horses, they would have to press on.

The trouble was, the two were out of food except for a little coffee and sugar. Worse, although they hunted separately neither was able to bag a deer or goose. Apparently the Pawnees had killed off all the game within miles. So Jim and the scout really had no choice. They had to locate the village or perish. "My companion was worn out," Jim said, "and seemed almost disheartened." Then he added stoutly, "I was young, and did not feel much the worse."

Fortunately, the next day Jim killed an elk. "He was exceedingly poor. Hungry as we were, we made a very unsavory supper off his flesh." Harris cut the surplus meat into strips and slow-cooked them over the fire. These and weak coffee made with muddy river water were all they had for the next five days as they traveled downstream. There was almost no wood along this stretch, so Harris made his fire of dried buffalo droppings. Nearly white from years of exposure, light as a feather, these age-old deposits from the buffalo, called chips, burned like charcoal with a bright fire and little smoke.

Jim had never known hunger before, but now he lived with the constant gnawing pain of it. After the dried meat was eaten, they staggered on another five days with no food at all. Jim was worried because his strength was failing. Harris, a much older man, could hardly put one foot ahead of the other. To save energy they discarded the coffee pot and skillet, then the canvas bags. Only the grim determination to survive kept them going. But finally Harris sank to the ground, moaning he could go no further. Jim hastily built a fire and wrapped him in all the blankets. He knew that if he lingered long with the scout, both would perish. But when he told Harris he must leave to find the Pawnees, Harris pleaded, "Don't leave me here to die!"

Nevertheless Jim gathered extra fuel and set out alone. He was so weak that he could not carry the rifle cradled in his arm and used it instead as a cane to keep from falling. The wind felt like a cold whip across his back. Still, he stubbornly put one foot forward, and then the other, and painfully advanced mile after mile.

Hours later he stopped to rest. As he squinted across the snowy plain, he thought he saw some dark figures moving far ahead. Praying they were Pawnee hunters, he fired a shot in the air. Seconds later he saw the figures halt. He fired a second shot and then stood spraddle-legged and reeling until three Indians reined up at his side. They were friendly but had no food with them. With much grunting they lifted Jim onto one of the horses so he could ride double with the owner.

When the rescuers turned their horses east, Jim protested. Somehow he made them understand about Harris. After some talk one Indian sped eastward, and the other two and Jim rode west. When they found Harris, he was unconscious. For the time being there was nothing to do but build up the fire and stay until help came from the Indian village.

Jim said, "After waiting about three hours, the rattling of hoofs was heard. Looking up, we discovered a troop of Indians approaching us at full speed. In another moment they were by our side. They brought with them a portion of light food, consisting of corn meal made into a kind of gruel."

Harris revived and began to eat the corn meal gruel the Indians had brought.

Jim reached frantically for the food, but the Indians allowed him only a spoonful. When he retained it, they let him sip a little more. Meanwhile others had roused Harris and were feeding him. Inside an hour Harris was able to sit up, and not long after said he could ride. Both he and Jim were helped onto horses and rode double to the Indian village. As soon as they were settled comfortably inside a tepee, Indian women brought them a kettle of stew. The two ate their fill, then lay back on the warm buffalo robes and slept soundly.

The next morning Harris found out through sign language and the few words of English which the Indians had learned from white traders, that they were members of the Oto tribe. They had no horses to sell, but since they were bound for the Ely and Curtis trading post with their furs, they would be glad to have their guests travel with them.

Jim and Harris talked over their situation. They would surely die if they tried to continue to the Pawnee camp. Probably by this time General Ashley had decided the two had perished and had proceeded without them. The wise thing to do was to accompany the Otos back to the trading post.

Traveling with the Otos gave Jim a vastly different picture of Indians and their way of life. Until this moment he knew them only as savages who had slain his family's neighbors, or as beggars who frequented the St. Louis waterfront. Now he saw them as *people* who had adapted skillfully to a semi-nomadic way of life. The village was noisy with the sound of children playing and dogs barking. There was much laughter and joking and visiting from lodge to lodge. The men invited Jim to sit and smoke with them or join in hunting, racing, or shooting contests. Jim marveled at their finely wrought bows and arrows, saddles and bridles. After the first few days, he got used to the flea-ridden tepees and dirt and enjoyed himself.

When they reached the post weeks later, Jim and Harris learned that General Ashley had given them up for dead and continued on to the mountains. The two white men who operated the post, Ely and Curtis, rewarded the Indians for treating Jim and Harris so well. They told the two that if they would do odd jobs about the place, they were welcome to stay until spring. Both accepted the offer.

Spring comes early to the lower Missouri River. As soon as the river was free of ice, Jim took passage on a steamer to St. Louis. After a quick run, he arrived there early in the evening of the fifth day.

When he first returned home, Jim vowed he would never leave his family again. He enjoyed being the center of attraction and entertaining his brothers and sisters with tales of his experiences. But shortly after, Jim became restless. Farm life seemed awfully dull. When his father urged him to return to his blacksmith's trade and settle down, Jim didn't like the prospect at all. The work was too confining for a man who had had a taste of adventure on the frontier.

Besides, he still wanted to see the Rocky Mountains. So he began wondering if General Ashley had returned to St. Louis and might be organizing another expedition. The only way to find out was to hurry to the big city. The sooner the better!

Jim didn't wait for his mother to prepare a going-away celebration. He said goodbye to everyone and raced off light-heartedly to St. Louis.

4

Wolf's Tail
and Buffalo Horn

"Shortly after my arrival I fell in with General Ashley, who had returned to the city for more men. The general was greatly surprised to see me. He had concluded that my fate had been the same as hundreds of others engaged to fur companies, who had perished with cold and starvation."

Although the new expedition had left St. Louis, the general sent Jim off on a fast horse to catch up with it. Once more he rode westward to the big bend in the Missouri River. Since it was early May, the weather was balmy and the air fragrant with spring blossoms. When Jim stopped briefly at the Ely and Curtis trading post, he learned that Ashley's men were headed for the Platte and Moses Harris had joined them. Jim had no difficulty tracking the outfit.

This third expedition of the Rocky Mountain Fur Company numbered 120 men and three times that many horses and mules. The trail of droppings and blackened firepits was easily followed.

When Jim finally caught up, Harris greeted him like an old friend and introduced him to the leader, Tom Fitzpatrick. Two years of trapping in the mountains had changed Fitzpatrick from a green hand into an extremely competent trapper and pathfinder. A good-looking, dark-haired fellow, he already bore scars of encounters with hostile Indians and a bear. Since he was one of the few Ashley employees who could read and write, the general soon trusted him with the firm's trapping and trading activities in the Wind River Mountains, in present Wyoming. Then after the party led by Fitzpatrick and Jed Smith located South Pass and discovered a vast unexplored mountainous region farther west in the Green River watershed, the general decided to send his third expedition into that region, with Fitzpatrick in charge. The firm had to expand because Ashley's partner, Andrew Henry, was not shipping down enough pelts from the trading post at the mouth of the Yellowstone.

Jim got right to work shoeing horses. He soon learned that most of his companions were greenhorns to whom he was a hero because of the experiences he had shared with Moses Harris. The younger fellows treated him with respect. This pleased him enormously. But instead of treating them with contempt, as Harris did, Jim went out of his way to be helpful.

That night several gathered around the fire while Jim told his version of the past winter's journey. When his listeners leaned breathlessly toward him and hung on every word, Jim couldn't resist embroidering the tale a bit here and there. He acted out the desperate hours before the Indians came to the rescue. He showed how he eyed the pretty Indian girls, and how he enjoyed sleeping in the tepee—until the fleas took over! His comrades burst into laughter and declared he was the best storyteller they had ever heard.

Jim soon learned that traveling overland under Tom Fitzpatrick's leadership was vastly different than under General Ashley's direction. The company functioned as if it were a military outfit moving into enemy territory. Since it was too large for all to eat together, the men were divided into messes. Each mess consisted of eight to ten men. It was represented by a leader who received the daily food ration for his mess mates from the clerk in charge of supplies. The mess leader had numerous duties. He had to see to it that the food was cooked properly, that his men cleaned their guns every night and kept them loaded at all times, that each took proper care of his riding horse and correctly loaded the pack animals in his care.

Thanks to the skills Jim had learned earlier, he was named leader for one mess. Very quickly he noticed that the men who broke camp speedily in the morning and were ready to travel before the others, earned the privilege of riding at the head of the column, where there was the least dust. From that moment on Jim determined his mess mates would occupy that cherished lead position. But instead of bossing them or forcing them into increased effort, Jim inspired them by the way he worked. Soon all took as much pride as Jim did in their conduct. For the remainder of the journey "Beckwourth's men" seldom lost their favorite place in the column.

When traveling, the company strung out for more than two miles with the men riding as guards for the entire length. Fitzpatrick, Harris and two or more hunters rode far in advance. They searched out and blazed the best route, and located a grassy camp-site for each night stop. Whenever possible this was near water. As soon as the column reached the site in the late afternoon, it formed a circle large enough to enclose all the animals. After Fitzpatrick pointed out the position each mess was to occupy, the animals were unloaded and led off to graze nearby under the watchful eyes of the horse guards. Next the men in each mess formed a breastwork of their packs and saddles, for protection should Indians attack. If the weather was bad, they raised small shelters of brush and mud and covered these with blankets or ground cloths. Then some gathered fire-wood and hauled water while Jim and the mess cook obtained the day's ration of flour, salt, sugar, coffee, and freshly killed wild game, which the advance party had provided. After supper all cleaned their guns and repaired any equipment damaged during the day's ride. Before dark they brought the livestock inside the circle where they were more secure from Indian raids. When all the chores were finished, the men might purchase a little tobacco or a swig of whiskey from the clerk, who charged the cost against their earnings. Then they were free to lounge about their campfires until turning in for the night.

Night guard duty was a necessity as the company traveled up the Platte River valley. Even though the Pawnees were considered "friendlies," they were accomplished horse thieves. In fact, many of the horses they traded to other tribes or sold to white men were stolen animals. To prevent their driving off the livestock at night, Tom Fitzpatrick posted guards at opposite ends of the camp. Guard duty was divided into three watches: from approximately eight o'clock at night to eleven, eleven to two in the morning, and two until daylight.

Shortly after Jim joined the company, he drew

the second watch. He managed some sleep before being awakened, and then with gun in hand he walked quietly around his sleeping comrades to a spot about three hundred yards out. Although the glow from the small campfires was a cheerful and reassuring sight, Jim felt very much alone in the midst of the limitless prairie. He looked hard about to be sure no Indians were skulking in the darkness. He listened until his ears ached, but all he heard was the animals grazing or the men snoring. There was no wind. The air was so clear and dry that Jim vowed he could hear the stars crackling overhead. For a long period he was absolutely motionless. Then he moved about cautiously, teaching himself to step soundlessly as an Indian, even though he was wearing thick-soled boots. He had heard Tom Fitzpatrick say that a trapper's chances of surviving in Indian country depended on his ability to learn the Indians' skills, and then out-perform them. This Jim determined to do.

Some time later Jim was positive he heard a rustling sound nearby. Then a twig snapped! Jim raised his gun and held his breath while he strained to identify the sound. Cold chills prickled up and down his spine, and perspiration beaded his forehead. He sniffed like a dog scenting danger, and the hair on his scalp stiffened.

Suddenly, in the faint glow of the firelight he saw

several dark shapes streaking toward the camp. It was a pack of wolves rushing in to kill a horse. The moment they started tearing one to bits, the horse's screams would stampede the entire herd over the bodies of the sleeping men. Jim fired three shots quickly. He saw one beast leap skyward and fall writhing to the ground. The pack slowed, and as the men in camp bolted out of their blankets and started shouting and firing their guns skyward, the wolves raced off, howling and snapping their jaws. Jim stayed at his post until all was quiet again, and the fires were built up to ward off any further attacks. But the moment the next guard relieved him, Jim ran to the dead wolf and cut off its tail. For the rest of the journey he kept it tied to the back of his saddle.

Jim explained further in his book, "Fur companies in those days had to depend upon their rifles for a supply of food. No company could possibly carry provisions sufficient to last beyond the most remote white settlements. We were now in buffalo country, but the Indians had driven them all away."

By the time Ashley's men approached the forks of the Platte River, the men were on very short rations. "Our allowance was half a pint of flour a day per man, which we made into a kind of gruel. If we happened to kill a duck or goose, it was shared as fairly as possible." After several more days during which the men saw no game worth a charge of powder, Fitzpatrick made an early stop. He announced that any man who wished to hunt was free to leave camp. Jim seized his rifle and took off at once on foot. "At the distance of a mile from the camp I came across a narrow deer trail through some brush. Directly across the trail not more than fifty yards distant, I saw a large fine buck standing. I did not wait for a nearer shot. I fired, and broke his back. I dispatched him by drawing my knife across his throat, and having partially dressed him, hung him on a tree close by. Proceeding onward I met a large white wolf. I shot him. Before I returned, I succeeded in killing three good-sized elk. I then returned near enough to the camp to signal to them to come to my assistance. All who were able turned out to my summons."

Then Jim added, with the good-humored boasting that was to become a trademark of his, "The game being all brought into camp, the fame of 'Jim Beckwourth' was celebrated by all."

Soon after this episode General Ashley arrived with a small party and took over the leadership. Since the men were still hungry, he sent them hunting again. A short distance from camp Jim killed two deer. Then, he added, "I perceived a large dark-colored animal grazing on the side of a hill, some mile and a half distant. I was determined to have a shot at him, whatever he might be. I knew meat was in demand, and that fellow, well stored, was worth more than a thousand teal ducks.

"I therefore approached with the greatest precaution to within fair rifle shot distance, scrutinizing him very closely, and still unable to make out what he was. I could see no horns. If he was a bear, I thought him an enormous one. I took sight at him over my faithful rifle, and then set it down to contemplate the huge animal still further. Finally I resolved to let fly. Taking good aim, I pulled the trigger. The rifle cracked, and I then made a rapid retreat toward the camp. After running about two hundred yards, and hearing no movement behind me, I ventured to look around. To my great joy, I saw the animal had fallen."

When he reached camp General Ashley asked if he had shot anything. Jim replied that he had shot two deer "and something else." What the "something else" was, Jim didn't know. The general brought out a pair of strong field glasses and exclaimed, "A buffalo, by heavens!"

Jim whooped for joy. He had heard men talk about shooting buffalo but had never seen one in the flesh. Small wonder he hadn't recognized the lumbering beast. Of course his friends teased him mercilessly, but none laughed harder than Jim. When the general ordered him and his mess mates to take a couple of horses and bring the meat into camp, Jim reported that he "suggested that two horses could not carry the load. Six were therefore dispatched, and they all came back well packed with his remains. There was great rejoicing throughout the camp. The two deer were also brought in, besides a fine one killed by the general, and ducks, geese, and such like were freely added by the other hunters."

Now Jim had a second trophy to tie on his saddle because he cut off one of the beast's horns and hung it alongside the wolf's tail.

That night when Jim pulled one of the roasted buffalo hump ribs from the fire and salted it, he declared the tender juicy meat the most delicious he had ever eaten. He didn't realize it, but now that he had two trophies to his credit and was enjoying his first meal of buffalo hump, he was on the threshold of becoming a mountain man.

5

On Top of the World

Twenty miles farther upriver Ashley and his men reached a Pawnee village. The Indians welcomed them with a feast and night-long dance. Then, Jim said, "We purchased for our future use beans, pumpkin, corn, cured meat, besides some beaver skins, giving them in exchange a variety of manufactured goods." Jim helped select the horses which the general also purchased. He hoped to resume travel the next day but the chief, Two Axe, objected.

"My men are about to surround the buffalo," Two Axe explained. "If you go now, you will frighten them. You must stay four days more. Then you may go."

Since the chief's word was law, Ashley obeyed. His men were delighted, especially Jim, because all wanted to join in the buffalo "surround."

Very early the next morning the warriors and fur men saddled up and rode quietly several miles until they sighted a large herd of buffalo. Two Axe, master of the hunt, signaled for the hunters to swing left and right and cautiously encircle the herd. Jim watched the Indians carefully. When the sun flooded the plain, they slipped off their buckskin shirts, drew arrows from the quivers strapped across their backs, and fitted these to their handsome powerful bows. Jim dismounted quickly, tightened the saddle girth and dropped his jacket and hat on the ground. He tied a rag over his hair to keep it from falling in his eyes. Then he remounted and loaded his rifle. Although quivering with suppressed excitement, he kept firm control of his horse, who was tossing its head.

Moments later a wild yipping sound flashed around the circle. Two Axe had shouted for the surround to begin. Every hunter relayed the signal and then slammed his heels into his horse's flanks. From all sides the hunters raced in on the doomed animals. By this time the great shaggy bulls, who weighed close to a ton apiece, were snorting and pawing large chunks of ground, and lowering their heads to charge. The cows bawled loudly for their calves, and bolted toward the center.

The hunters raced in on the doomed animals.

Yelling like an Indian, Jim kept pace with those each side of him. When he got within shooting range, he wrapped the reins around the saddle horn, pressed his knees hard against the horse, and raised the rifle with both hands. Even as he started firing, the dust was whirling about him, and clods of dirt hit him in the face. The noise was almost terrifying in its savage mixture of shooting, yowling, and animals roaring in defiance and pain. Jim kept yelling and firing as the others did, until the ground was strewn with wounded and dead animals. By this time his horse's flanks were heaving, its hide lathered with foam. It stumbled to a halt, almost pitching Jim to the ground. Then he waited until the shooting petered out and it was safe to dismount. The plain looked like a vast slaughterhouse.

After a brief period of shouting and bragging up their kills, the Indians began to strip off the hides and cut out the choice portions of meat. Jim claimed fourteen hundred buffalo had been killed. "The tongues were counted by General Ashley himself."

The Indians would devote several weeks to curing the hides and preserving the meat for winter. But Ashley was anxious to leave. As Jim said, "The 'surround' accomplished, we received permission from Two Axe to take up our line of march. Accordingly, we started along the river, and had only proceeded five miles from the village when we found that the Platte forked. Taking the south fork, we journeyed on some six miles, when we encamped. So we continued every day, making slow progress, until we had left the Pawnee village three hundred miles in our rear. We found plenty of buffalo along our route until we approached the Rocky Mountains when the buffalo, as well as all other game became scarce, and we had to resort to the beans and corn supplied us by the Pawnees."

It was December now, bitterly cold. The snow lay deep in the valley. The poor horses had only the soft bark of cottonwood trees to eat. When blizzards screamed down the east slope of the mountains, the men sat out the storms wrapped in blankets and hunched before their campfires. But the severe weather also drove the elk and deer down from the high country. Before long the men had meat aplenty. The enforced rest also renewed their strength. In a few weeks the expedition slowly floundered northward into present-day Wyoming and began the long slow ascent of South Pass. The going was easier because the broad, low saddle was almost devoid of trees, and the wind blew off much of the snow.

Jim slogged along on foot now, head down to watch his footing, leading his weakened riding horse and two pack mules. He felt no strain of climbing in his sturdy legs. But at long last he and his mess mates felt no more pull on their knees. They looked up and then hollered joyfully. The ground no longer rose ahead of them. Instead it dropped away gently. They had reached the summit!

Although icy peaks glowered down on all sides, the men felt as if they were on top of the world. The long column straggled to a halt as the exuberant men cavorted about in the snow, tossed their hats in the air, and shouted themselves hoarse. Grinning broadly, Tom Fitzpatrick pulled an axe from a saddle sling and chopped a large hole in a creek. Jim hovered at his side and whooped as he saw that the water was running downhill, *toward the west*. Now he truly knew what it meant to stand on the high backbone of the Continental Divide. Behind him, the waters flowed eastward to the Missouri and Mississippi rivers. But the stream trickling at his feet was Pacific Creek, so-named because its waters flowed into the Green River, whose emerald flood swelled the Colorado and after winding through awesome mile-deep canyons eventually flowed into the Gulf of California and the Pacific Ocean.

Actually, Jim and his companions had little interest in geography. They weren't explorers. They were trappers, far more intent on the beaver swarming along the westbound streams because their livelihood depended on trapping them. And, more immediately, they were overjoyed at the sight of thousands of buffalo seen grazing far off in a broad valley cut by the sparkling green river. So they all whooped again when General Ashley told them that the valley was their goal, the end of their long and rugged journey.

Another month passed before this third expedition of the Rocky Mountain Fur Company came to rest beside the Green River. By this time the snow had melted from the wild grass at the lower elevation, and the willows had sprouted tender shoots and pale yellow leaves. The horses were staked out and allowed to fill their shrunken stomachs. While some of the men gathered wood for crackling bonfires and raised temporary shelters of brush, the best shooters went hunting. They scattered in groups of two and three. Jim found himself accompanying General Ashley, who was an excellent shot. Not long after, the general wounded a buffalo, a huge bull. It sank slowly onto its knees. But when the general unwisely moved toward it on foot, the beast suddenly lunged to its feet and bore down on him. It knocked him down and tried to gore him with its sharp horns. In the few seconds this had happened, Jim had raised his rifle. But he had to hold his fire for the one killing shot that would hit the animal and not the general. Finally he fired. The buffalo jerked convulsively and began to slump. The general rolled away frantically before the heavy body crashed to the ground. After he scrambled to his feet, little the worse for the narrow escape, he embraced Jim and told him he was deeply grateful for having rescued him from certain death.

Then, Jim continued, "After remaining in camp four or five days, the general resolved upon dividing our party into detachments of four or five men each, and sending them on different routes, in order the better to accomplish the object of our perilous journey which was collecting all the beaver skins possible."

Perhaps because the general was grateful for being rescued, but more likely because Jim consistently had proved to be a top hand, the general "mentioned to Fitzpartick that I ought to have the lead of a party. He believed I was as capable as any one in the company for it."

But Jim refused the honor. He reminded Ashley and Fitzpatrick that he had never trapped, that this was his first trip to the mountains, and that he felt he still had a great deal to learn. Also, he said there were older men more deserving of the important responsibility.

It is a rare man who will admit to lack of experience and be willing to accept a secondary post in order to learn a complicated and dangerous business. But Jim Beckwourth was such a man. His refusal increased the older men's respect for their Negro comrade. Fitzpatrick then assigned Jim to a small brigade of six men whose leader was an exceedingly able former Kentuckian, named Clements.

After all the trapping parties received their traps, guns and ammunition, camping gear, and other supplies, the general called for a farewell celebration. He opened a jug of brandy and treated all the men to several drinks, as well as portions of tobacco. He praised them for their loyalty and bravery and ordered all to come together at this site the first week in July. Meanwhile he would have made a fast trip back to St. Louis and returned with thousands of dollars worth of trade goods and supplies.

When he concluded, the men doffed their caps and cheered the general lustily. Then one man brought out a mouth organ, and another a fiddle. The men began to sing. Some leaped up to jig. With hair and beards and heels flying, they danced under the starbright sky. In the morning they waved off the general and his party and said goodby all around. Then all rode out from the campsite toward the Green River and its tributary creeks for the spring hunt.

6

Jim Becomes a Trapper

"Our route was up the river—a country that none of us had ever seen before—where the foot of the white man had seldom, if ever, left its print. We were very successful in finding beaver as we progressed, and we obtained plenty of game for the wants of our small party."

Jim quickly learned that beaver prefer deep calm water and labor diligently to raise a dam of sticks and mud to stop the flow of a creek or spring in order to create a pond. First they felled many small trees, using their large sharp front teeth to gnaw through the soft wood. After chopping off the branches, they dragged the pieces to the water and began building the dam, which contained their home, of sticks and mud. The entrance to their lodge was under water, but the main chamber inside the dam was a foot above water. Here, in small dark chambers the adults spent the winter months, and the kits were born and raised. The family lived off the soft bark of the branches stored at the base of the dam. As soon as the pond ice melted, the family resumed its busy work of felling more trees and gathering the next winter's food supply.

Knowing Jim had never trapped, Clement took great pains to teach him. Trapping beaver called for considerable skill and great patience. Each man in the party had been given five iron traps, each weighing five pounds, which he carried in a sack. Jim learned to set them either along the beaver's land route to and from the water, or under water downstream from the dam. To do the latter, Jim had to wade into icy water above his knees, cautiously place the trap close by the bank and anchor it with a stick driven into the bottom. The "bait" was another stick dipped in a vial containing a musky secretion taken from the glands of a beaver. Lured by the powerful scent, the animal was drawn to the trap. When it closed on his foot, the weight held the animal under water until it drowned.

Jim checked his "line" every day or so, removed the dead beavers, and reset the traps. On returning to camp, he skinned the carcasses, scraped the flesh side clean, stretched the pelt on a circular hoop and dried it in the sun. When he had accumulated sixty skins, he bundled these together into a *plew*. His and his comrades' plews were then cached, or hidden, in dry underground pits so they would not be stolen by Indians. After all the beaver from one area were trapped out, the trappers moved on to another stream, and another.

"In a very few days we succeeded in taking over one hundred beaver, the skins of which were worth ten dollars per pound in St. Louis." Jim worked extra hard because General Ashley had promised each man a bonus for every pelt procured over a quota of about one hundred or more skins per man.

One day when the trappers returned to their camp, they found sixteen Indians nosing around their belongings. While they appeared friendly, the trappers watched them carefully and shared their food and a little tobacco with them. After dark all rolled in their blankets or robes except a man named La Brache, who stood guard by the fire. He kept the fire burning brightly. Jim and his comrades fell asleep "when we were all suddenly startled by a loud cry from Le Brache and the instant report of a gun. We were all up in an instant. An Indian seized my rifle, but I wrenched it from him."

Jim had the presence of mind to scatter the ashes of the fire with the butt of his rifle, "to prevent the Indians from making a sure mark of us." Within seconds the Indians had dived into some brush and were firing on the trappers. They, in turn, threw themselves flat and returned the attack. By forming a ring and placing their shots carefully, they held off their attackers until daylight. Then, surprisingly, the Indians quit the fight and disappeared. The trappers hastily buried Le Brache, who had been tomahawked, packed their belongings, and moved to a site more easily defended. Fortunately, their enemies did not return.

The life of a trapper was one of unceasing hardship and danger. They had to hunt for meat, gather firewood, and cook. Most ran out of flour very soon and subsisted on wild game and water. Their meager stores of salt, coffee, and tobacco were doled out pinch by pinch. The men ate lightly on rising and slipped out in twos and threes to set their traps. None dared make a careless or noisy move for fear of attracting Indians.

In the late afternoon the weary men, hands and feet aching from the hours spent in cold water, trudged back to camp to do their chores. Each ate about eight pounds of meat daily, stuffing himself at night like a snake who has swallowed a frog. Then they lounged about the fire, rifle at hand, sipping coffee or hot water, and enjoying a well-earned rest. But nights are long in the mountains. To pass the time and fight off the depression brought on by their being so far from home, the men entertained each other with storytelling. The same story might be repeated so many times that the listeners would forget who told it originally and think the story was theirs. Thus Jim added to his small store of exciting and funny incidents and gradually sharpened his talent as an effective spinner of yarns.

Ashley's men were not the only ones in the field. A dozen other American firms and two British outfits had men ranging throughout the Rocky Mountains. These small parties pressed farther and farther into unexplored country until they knew the mountainous heartland of North America. Only a few, such as Lieutenant Zebulon Pike or Captain John Charles Fremont, gained lasting fame for their efforts. But even they relied heavily on friendly Indians and American mountain men to lead them to their great discoveries. Many mountain men died in the high country and were buried in unmarked graves. The bruising winter cold, chilling spring rains, starvation, accidents, pneumonia, and malnutrition killed more than succumbed in attacks by Indians and bears. The terrible strain of being in constant danger took its toll of sanity, too, and some men lost their minds.

Yet despite all these hardships and dangers, many young men like Jim Beckwourth remained trappers until the beautiful animals were trapped almost to extinction, and fickle fashion discarded beaver hats for silk ones. But while the young men were still vigorous, like Jim they vowed there was no better life for a man who wanted to be wholly free in spirit, mind, and action. Throughout his book, Jim recalled the spicy aroma of pine forests, the clear sweet creek waters, starbright nights, mountain meadows carpeted with flowers in summer, the slopes blazing with golden leaves in the fall, the joy of penetrating into remote canyons where no civilized man had set foot before, the close comradeships, and once seasoned, the great pride in having solidly earned the respect and admiration of the most accomplished frontiersmen on the continent.

Clement, the leader of Jim's party, kept track of the passing days by tying knots in a string. When it was mid-June and his men had hundreds of pelts, he led the way back to the Green River for the great rendezvous. By the first week in July they had revisited their camps, retrieved the furs from the caches, and brought them on mule and horseback to the handsome valley. As each party trouped in, those already in camp greeted the members with shouts and backslapping. After a brief pause to brag up their accomplishments and tell how Le Brache "went under," Clement and his men delivered their peltries to General Ashley.

The general had moved a long train of pack horses

and mules bearing $75,000 worth of trade goods across the 2,700 miles from St. Louis to the Green River. Since word of his coming had spread throughout the mountains, many free trappers who worked independently and hundreds of Indians brought their furs to trade for guns, hardware, clothing, liquor, tobacco, and imported foods. The Indians were a mixed group of Cheyennes, Snakes, Nez Perces, Crows, and others. They flowed into the valley in a colorful parade of warriors, squaws, children, horses, dogs and horse-drawn travois, or skin drags, used to transport household belongings. Each band camped off by itself, raising their tepees near the river. Then each paraded throughout the entire campsite to display the gorgeous buckskin shirts, leggings, and dresses, the beaded and feathered bonnets, war shields, quivers, and buffalo robes. Every afternoon there were horse races, wrestling matches, marksmanship contests, singing, dancing, and gambling. At night after gorging on meat slathered with thick gravy and biscuits dripping with molasses, everyone danced and drank whisky until dawn.

Jim described the rendezvous thus: "We constituted quite a little town, numbering at least eight hundred souls, of whom one half were women and children. There was some among us who had not seen any groceries, such as coffee, sugar, etc., for several months. The whisky went off as freely as water. All kinds of sports were indulged in with a heartiness that would astonish more civilized societies."

After General Ashley paid his men their salaries and bonuses, they splurged for blanket cloth jackets, hats and boots, guns, knives, pickles, candy, and hundreds of other items. The men also bought beads, mirrors, kettles, needles, and bolts of bright calico to trade to the Indian women for their handsome buckskin shirts and beaded moccasins. Many mountain men who had already married Indian women treated their wives to cheap jewelry, feathers, and face paint. At the close of two weeks trading, the general had sold every scrap of his trade goods and had acquired 190 packs, or plews, of 60 peltries each. In St. Louis each plew would enrich him by $1,000. However, not all packs were made up of beaver fur. A good many included the skins of grey and white wolves, mink, marten, fox, and bears.

Jim said, "There lay the general's fortune in one immense pile, collected at the expense of severe toil, privation, suffering, peril, and in some cases, loss of life. If he should meet with no misfortune on his way to St. Louis, he would receive enough to pay all his debts, and have an ample fortune besides."

Most of the trappers and Indians disappeared into the mountains for another year of trapping. But Jim was chosen by the general to be one of twenty hunters and guards for the long journey east. Somewhere along the way Jim and a man named Baptiste were hunting. They killed and butchered a buffalo. Heading back to camp, Baptiste rode in the lead with a great haunch of meat tied to the back of his saddle. When he stopped to let his horse drink in a creek, a grizzly bear reared up in a thicket. The horse, frightened by its growl, bucked Baptiste to the ground and raced off. The grizzly pounced on the poor man.

At that moment Jim rode onto the scene. His horse screamed and unseated him. This distracted the grizzly momentarily, so Jim had time to cock his rifle and kill the beast with one shot. Poor Baptiste! He was horribly lacerated. Jim ran towards camp, shouting for help. His comrades responded and helped bring the badly mauled man back to camp.

"Soon after reaching camp we heard a great rush of horses, and perceived a party of Indians charging directly toward our camp, and driving before them another bear of enormous size. All the camp scattered and took to trees. I was standing by the wounded man, and became so terrified that I hardly knew whether I was standing on the ground or was

The grizzly pounced on Baptiste.

in a tree. Every man was calling to me, 'To a tree, Jim! To a tree!' "

But the moment the bear scented Baptiste's blood, it slowed and ambled toward him. Jim streaked toward his rifle and managed to kill the beast before it harmed Baptiste.

Once more Jim found himself a hero. Since he was an employee of Ashley's, the general had the right to claim the skins, which would sell readily at St. Louis. The men welcomed a feast of fat bear meat, and praised Jim for his marksmanship and daring. But Jim felt he came out the real winner when he was allowed to cut off one giant grizzly paw and make a necklace of the long sharp claws.

By some miracle, Baptiste recovered from his mauling. The cavalcade reached St. Louis on October 8, 1825. Jim described the homecoming this way. "When we came in sight of the city we were saluted by a piece of artillery, which continued its discharges until we landed at the market-place. There were not less than a thousand persons present, who hailed our arrival with shouts which deafened our ears. Such a rushing, crowding, pulling, hauling, weeping, and laughing I had never before witnessed. Every one had learned of our approach by courier. My father, who had moved to St. Louis, was in the crowd, and was overjoyed to see me."

Of course, Jim had dressed for the occasion.

Although he says nothing about it, one wonders how Jim's father and the rest of the family reacted when they saw this big-muscled man, black hair curling on his shoulders and bushy beard hiding his chin, broad shoulders bulging under a buckskin shirt overlaid with a necklace of bear claws. The youth who had been gone from home so long had come back not a man, but a *mountain man.*

7

Outwitting the Blackfeet

"I had been in St. Louis only one week when General Ashley desired me to return to the mountains immediately, to carry dispatches to Mr. W. L. Sublette, captain of the trappers."

Jim did not hesitate when the general offered him $1,000 to make this trip. He would not travel alone since the general also hired two others, at far less money, to accompany him.

Since $1,000 was considered a small fortune in those days, Jim jumped at the offer. That sum would go a long way toward buying a farm, or setting himself up in the blacksmith business, or acquiring a home when he finally settled down to married life. At least, this was his thinking when he left the next day on what he expected to be a quick trip to the mountains.

Jim and his companions rode hard day after day. Once they put the Republican River behind them, they proceeded with extreme caution in order not to attract any Indians. They always halted before dark to build a fire and eat. But after dark they quietly moved on to another site well hidden in the trees or underbrush. They lighted no fire, breakfasted on cold meat and biscuit before sunrise, and pressed on.

It was late November before they reached the Green River. Here they met a small party of trapper friends who told them Bill Sublette had chosen a site further west, near present Ogden, Utah, to serve as winter quarters. So instead of delivering his dispatches and hurrying back to St. Louis, Jim rode deeper into the mountains. Sublette's choice was an excellent one. He had several log cabins built at the foot of the west slope of the Wasatch Mountains, close by an enormous body of salt water called Great Salt Lake. Winter temperatures and snowfall were less severe here, and thousands of wild game and waterfowl in the area assured a good food supply. By the time all the trapping parties came in and a large encampment of Snake Indians settled down, Jim said their community numbered from six to seven hundred souls, including the Indian women and children.

Jim shared a cabin with Tom Fitzpatrick, Jim Bridger, Moses Harris, and others. After an Indian woman cooked their supper, they sat about the fire-place spinning yarns. As the men talked, Jim realized bit by bit that he was far more comfortable here than in St. Louis, that he was far closer to these men and their way of life than he was to his relatives back home. So it wasn't hard to convince himself that he might enjoy another season of trapping with these good fellows.

By spring Jim reached a decision. Up to this time he looked upon trapping as a lark, a youthful adventure which bridged the period between his release from his apprenticeship and his settling down near his family in Missouri. Now he knew at first hand that trapping was a highly skilled endeavor which could turn him a profit. In other words, beaver spelled dollars to Jim. He also knew the tremendous profits to be realized if he became a trader. While he could never expect to be wealthy enough to form a company such as the general had, he could save the money earned from trapping, add it to the thousand dollars Ashley would pay him, and in a season or two have enough money to become a trader in the mountains.

When the ice melted from the mountain streams and lakes, the trapping parties headed out in all directions. Jim gladly accepted the post of brigade leader because now he felt ready for the responsibility. At first trapping was poor because the nearest streams were almost trapped out. This forced him to push northward into an unexplored jumble of peaks, canyons, and streams. Here the trapping was superb, but the dangers heightened because he was operating in range of the most warlike and hostile of all Rocky Mountain tribes, the Blackfeet.

One day after Jim set his trap line, he rode slowly to higher country, seeking new locations for his men to trap. Hours later he emerged from the timber out onto a sunlit mountain meadow, right smack into a camp of Blackfeet hunters. As they leaped for their bows and horses, Jim turned his mount, spurred hard, and streaked toward the mountain top. He wanted to draw the Indians away from his camp, and knowing several ridges probably joined at the summit, his only escape lay in turning off in a different direction.

His poor horse fought the rocky ground until it stumbled on a rock, and broke its foreleg. Jim jumped clear with his rifle and continued on foot. By the time he climbed several hundred feet, he heard the Indians yelping as they discovered his horse. Fortunately they stopped to kill the animal and apparently quarreled over who should have the saddle. Meantime Jim slipped through a crevice between some large boulders and covered himself with brush. Not long after, the Indians were swarming all around him, like angry ants. Often they were only a few yards from him. But after a long futile search, they left the scene.

Jim guessed they had returned to quarrel over his saddle, so he worked his way to the top of the mountain and loped down into another canyon. For two days he walked, hid, and walked, deliberately leaving traces of his passing, in hopes the Blackfeet would follow him and be drawn further and further from his men. The ruse worked. After several more days during which he was hungry but gleeful over his skill at outwitting his pursuers, he returned to his camp. His men wisely had secreted themselves while awaiting his return. Once reunited, all moved quickly over the mountain and resumed trapping in still another canyon.

In July Jim's brigade and all the others came together on the Green River. Jim said, "Mirth, songs, dancing, shouting, trading, running, jumping, singing, racing, target shooting, yarns, frolic, with all sorts of extravagances which white men or Indians could invent, were freely indulged in. The unpacking of the *medicine water* [liquor] contributed much to the heightening of our festivities."

At the close of the trading fair, General Ashley announced that he had sold out to Bill Sublette. He was rich now and would journey no more to the mountains. He thanked his men for their loyalty and good work, paid them off in gold and silver coins, and then led the long train of 300 mules, each laden with furs, back to St. Louis. Since Bill Sublette was well liked, most of the employees continued working for him. Jim said, "We spent the summer months at our leisure, trading with the Indians, hunting, sporting, and preparing for the fall harvest of beaver." The fat paddle-tailed animals were not trapped in the summer because their fur was in poor condition then.

During this time Jim traveled with a sixty-man brigade under the leadership of Bill Sublette. Since half the men brought along their Indian wives and children, the men were relieved of all camp chores. Because they were large in number and well armed, the Blackfeet mostly let them alone. But in a few forays, the trappers wiped out enough Indians so that each man, like Jim, had a scalp or two to tie onto his saddle.

Jim had no qualms about killing hostile Indians. To survive in the mountains, a man had to kill or be killed. He enjoyed the challenge of outwitting and outfighting his enemies and had no more hesitation about killing them than he had in killing a grizzly or buffalo. Jim was not alone in this attitude. While trappers became a closely knit brotherhood and often risked their lives for their comrades, as a group they felt they were involved in a deadly conflict with any Indian who posed a threat to their friends and families or their grim determination to reign as lords of the mountains.

One day Jim and a French-Canadian named Le Bleux, who had survived twenty years in the mountains, rode far out from camp. They came to the edge of a bluff. The downslope was very steep and rocky and choked with dense underbrush. Some thirty feet below flowed a broad sparkling river. As they paused on the brink, they heard noises far to their rear. Suddenly a party of Indian raiders rode into view. They were Blackfeet. They spied the trappers, whooped, and raced toward them.

Jim and his friend forced their horses over the edge and down into a thicket where they were hidden from sight. Le Bleux's horse had a small bell attached to its neck. Le Bleux took this off, and crawling on to a distant bush, fastened the bell there with one end of his long rawhide lariat. Then he and Jim scuttled on still further until Le Bleux had played out the entire length of the rope. When the Indians dismounted and peered over the bluff, Le Bleux pulled on the lariat, which made the bell tinkle. The Indians yelped and fired arrows into the brush. When the bell tinkled again, they flung more arrows in its direction.

Jim could not contain his laughter and guffawed loudly. Immediately some of the warriors ran along the bluff and fired down upon him. Jim and Le

Bleux stuck their rifle barrels through the brush hiding them, fired, ducked down and scuttled to another spot, and fired again. Then Le Bleux crawled back on hands and knees to give the bell rope another jerk. The Indians roared with rage, fired toward the bell and elsewhere without hitting the trappers.

While Jim enjoyed the trick, he knew they were outnumbered about twenty to two. He asked his companion what they should do. Le Bleux grinned and motioned Jim to follow. He eased down to the water's edge and slid into the cold water. Then he and Jim paddled close under the bank for more than a mile, only to discover the Indians had followed along and were on the bluff above them. Then Le Bleux motioned for Jim to swim for the opposite shore.

Jim took several deep breaths, submerged, and swam downstream as far as he could. Then he surfaced, gulped air, dove again, and gradually worked his way diagonally across the current to the far shore. Even though the Indians could not shoot that far, the trappers crawled up the bank and ran until they reached a point where, Jim said, "we could safely look back and laugh at our pursuers."

Not long after the two returned to the trappers' main camp, a Blackfeet war party attacked. Jim and Le Bleux had risen very early and saw the hostiles gathering at a distance. They roused their companions, and then Jim stepped out into the open and roared a challenge for the Indians to come on and fight. The Blackfeet charged. According to Jim, "When they saw us arise, rifles in hand, they drew back. Had they rushed on with their battle axes, they could have killed us in an instant."

Still, the Indians managed to kill some of the trappers' horses and mules and one of their men. Jim and his comrades used the bodies of the dead horses as breastworks, and in time their deadly accurate shooting thoroughly routed the enemy. But they left seventeen dead warriors behind. As soon as the trappers realized the fight was over, they leaped up, ran to the dead Indians, and scalped them. So now Jim had a fresh scalp to tie on his saddle and another suspenseful experience to add to his wealth of yarns.

Eventually the brigade worked its way northeastward to the headwaters of a river that was either the Powder or Big Horn. It flowed north, down from the mountains and out across a grassy plain toward the Yellowstone River, in present eastern Montana. This was the heart of the hunting grounds claimed by the Crow Indians, one of the most handsome and superior tribes in all America. Thousands of buffalo, elk, and antelope grazed on the golden native grass. The river and its tributary creeklets swarmed with beaver. To reap a rich harvest of furs, Sublette split his brigade into a dozen smaller outfits. The men could expect little trouble because the Crows had a solidly established reputation for being friendly to trappers.

So once more Jim set forth to trap in the tried and true way. Even in his wildest dreams he could never have imagined what lay ahead.

8

"...my Indian life with the Crows"

As Jim's brigade worked slowly northward toward the Yellowstone, he said, "It seemed a relief to be in a place where we could rest from our unsleeping vigilance, and to feel when we rose in the morning, there was some probability of our living till night."

One day some Crow hunters visited their camp. Fortunately one of Jim's men, Caleb Greenwood, was married to a Crow woman and spoke their language. After being treated to a hearty meal and some tobacco, the Indians drew a map on the ground to show where their new friends would find many beaver. Then Greenwood, to impress them, related how Sublette's large brigade had been attacked repeatedly by the Blackfeet, who were mortal enemies of the Crows. When Greenwood bragged that the trappers had killed hundreds and hundreds of Blackfeet (which they had not), the Crows leaped to their feet and danced for joy. Then they asked who among the trappers had killed the most Blackfeet.

Greenwood hesitated. Then with eyes sparkling and a roguish look in his eye, he said that Jim had!

The Crows hugged Jim and rubbed their cheeks against his. For a second Jim didn't know whether they were going to kiss him or kill him. Greenwood assured him they were expressing their pleasure.

Then Greenwood, who relished telling tall tales, pulled a whopper. He told the hunters that Jim was a Crow! Since Jim's skin was naturally a light brown but deeply suntanned, the Indians were not too surprised. But they did ask how this fact could be true. Greenwood obliged them with an elaborate fib. He asked them if they remembered many, many years ago when the Cheyenne Indians defeated the Crows, killing hundreds of the warriors and kidnapping a great many young women and children.

The Indians nodded. They remembered hearing their parents tell them about this black period in Crow history.

Then Greenwood declared, "Well, he [Jim] was a little boy at that time. The whites bought him off the Cheyennes. He has become a great brave among them, and all your enemies fear him."

"Ayee!" the Crows exclaimed, backing away from Jim as if he had just appeared from the spirit world. They leaped on their ponies and raced off to tell their people that a great Crow hero and killer of many Blackfeet had come back to them.

When Greenwood explained the joke to Jim he bent double with laughter. Neither of them thought any more about it and continued trapping.

Meanwhile, however, the Crow hunters had repeated the story all around their village. Immediately the old women who remembered the Cheyenne defeat began to wonder if Jim was the son they had lost during the raid. All expressed their desire to see this great hero. Obviously, from what happened later, they made plans to bring Jim to their village one way or another.

Not long after, Jim was out trapping alone, something he had rarely dared do before reaching Crow country. Soon he came onto a large herd of horses. By the time he realized they were not wild horses, he was surrounded by Indian horse guards. Positive they were Crows because they seemed especially happy to see him, Jim wasn't alarmed. In fact, he handed over his gun as a sign of his friendly feelings toward them. The guards marched him to the large

Surrounded by Indian horse guards, Jim handed over his gun as a sign of his friendly feelings toward them.

village nearby, right into the chief's tepee. This made Jim suspect that the Indians had been spying on his movements for some time and that his "capture" was not unexpected.

A village crier announced his arrival, and all the people streamed toward the chief's large tepee. Then, Jim said, when all was quiet inside, the hunters who had visited Jim's camp pointed at him and said, "That is the lost Crow, the great brave who has killed so many of our enemies. He is our brother." Fortunately one young brave spoke some English and told Jim what had been said.

Jim had to swallow hard to keep from laughing out loud. Also, he wasn't going to do anything that might anger the Crows.

Next the old women who had lost sons during the raid long ago were brought in. Jim said, "The old women, breathless with excitement, their eyes wild and protruding, and their nostrils dilated, arrived in squads, until the lodge was overflowing. I believe never was a mortal gazed at with such intense and sustained interest as I was on that occasion. Arms and legs were critically scrutinized. My face next passed the ordeal; then my neck, back, breast, even down to my feet."

At length one old crone said, "If this is my son, he has a mole just over his left eye!"

Jim continued, "My eyelids were immediately

pulled down. Sure enough, she discovered a mole just over my left eye!"

The woman cried, "He is my son!" The rest of her family crowded close to hug and touch Jim. Then he was swept out of the chief's lodge into another to meet his "father," whose name was Big Bowl. Here more relatives "seized me in their arms and hugged me, and my face positively burned with the enraptured kisses of my numerous fair sisters, with a long host of cousins, aunts, and other more remote kindred."

Big Bowl demanded quiet. Then he told all present that they must support and protect this long-lost son, whom he named Morning Star. He declared the Great Spirit had sent Morning Star back to his people so he could teach them how to defeat all their enemies. The relatives cheered and dispersed to prepare for a great celebration.

Next Jim's old clothes were stripped off and replaced with soft handsome buckskin leggings, shirt, and beaded moccasins fit for a great warrior. Then, laughingly, Jim was pushed out into the sunshine so the whole village could see how handsome he was.

Jim was having such a good time that he played his new role to the hilt. He flexed his muscles and strutted about, dancing and pantomiming how he had killed *hundreds* of Blackfeet. When he winked at some pretty young girls, they giggled and ran to hide. Not long after, Big Bowl summoned Jim back into the tepee for a serious talk. The interpreter was present, so Jim was able to learn what was expected of him.

The first rule laid down by his new father was that Jim must henceforth live with his Indian family. Jim didn't let on that he had no intention of doing so, for he understood that if ever he made any attempt to leave, he would be killed. As an adult male, he was expected to be a warrior and take part in battles against either the Cheyennes or Blackfeet. That Jim could accept because by this time he had developed a deep hatred for the latter.

With the interpreter's help, he explained that he was a trapper and must go away some day to turn his furs in to the "big chief" of the fur company. Big Bowl said this would not be necessary. The Crows knew all about trappers and fur companies. For decades Americans and Britishers had been permitted to trap in Crow country. They had traded the Crows many fine articles in exchange for the Indians' furs. So it would be all right if Jim continued trapping. There was a large new fur post near the mouth of the Yellowstone and Jim could go there whenever he had enough furs to trade.

Jim made sure his "father" knew that all this pleased him very much. In his heart he promised himself that some day, somehow, he would escape. But for now his life depended on acting as the Crows wished.

Next, Jim said, Big Bowl "suddenly demanded of me if I wanted a wife; thinking no doubt that if he got me married, I should lose all discontent and forego any wish of returning to the whites.

"I assented, of course."

"Very well," said Big Bowl, "you shall have a pretty wife and a good one." Away he strode to the lodge of one of the great braves and asked for one of his daughters to bestow on his son.

The girl's father let Jim choose from three young and very pretty girls. Jim chose the one whose name was Stillwater. Later he declared she deserved her name because she was "affectionate, obedient, gentle, and cheerful."

The marriage ceremony consisted of a discussion between Big Bowl and Stillwater's father to decide what gifts must be exchanged between them. When the terms were agreed on the young couple were declared husband and wife. Meantime Jim's "mother" and the older women had raised a tepee for their home and furnished it with soft buffalo robes and other household belongings. Next one of Jim's newly acquired brothers appeared with twenty fine horses. He presented these, explaining that a Crow warrior must have the swiftest, strongest horses and the best saddle and riding gear. Then another brother solemnly presented Jim with a superbly made bow, a beaded quiver filled with arrows, and a round war shield made of tough buffalo hide.

Thanks to the time Jim had spent among other tribes at the mountain rendezvous, he knew how to thank his family for their great generosity. He made a long speech in which he bragged about his exploits and promised to lead his people to a victory over their enemies. Then he and Stillwater led a procession which ended in a wild and joyous celebration.

Jim said, "Thus I commenced my Indian life with the Crows. I said to myself, 'I can trap in their streams unmolested, and derive more profit under their protection than if among my own men, exposed incessantly to assassination and alarm.' I therefore resolved to abide with them, to guard my secret, to do my best in their company, and assist them to subdue their enemies."

9

Chief of the Crow Nation

When Jim Beckwourth failed to return to his trapper friends, they decided he had been captured or killed by the Cheyenne Indians who preyed constantly on the Crows. Sorrowfully they said, "Poor Jim has gone under." Without their leader, they withdrew from the region and rejoined Sublette's brigade. So the word spread through the mountains that one of the best and bravest of mountain men was dead.

By this time Jim was riding north with a Crow war party bent on lifting Blackfeet scalps. After traveling many miles they sighted a party of eleven Blood Indians, who were a band of the Blackfeet nation. Immediately the Crow chief sounded the war cry and charged them. The Indian way of attacking was to make horrendous noises which were supposed to frighten the enemy, bear down on them while shooting, then divide and circle away to regroup and mount a second swift charge. Jim had seen this maneuver many times in the brushes he had had with other tribes. Thus he knew that the Indian habit of turning away, instead of wiping out a party on the first charge, had saved his life and those of his friends on many occasions. So, knowing that he must distinguish himself on this first raid with the Crows, if only to live up to his own and Greenwood's bragging, Jim fought "mountain man style."

When the Crows charged, he did too. But when they turned away, Jim rode right into the astonished Bloods, who were not used to close combat. He slipped his rifle into his saddle sling and started flailing away with his stone war axe. Seconds later he sank it into an enemy's skull. Even before this man dropped to the ground, Jim was striking at others.

When the Crows looked around, they saw their new brother in mortal close combat. In their eyes there was no more daring or dangerous conduct. Quickly they spurred their ponies, rode down on the Bloods, and helped finish off the entire party.

Jim's companions now regarded him with great awe, because he had so quickly tallied several *coups*, or war honors. To touch a live enemy was an honor; to kill one in close contact was a greater honor; to fight surrounded by enemies and emerge victorious was the greatest honor of all. Jim had done all these.

After gathering up the Blood's horses and belongings, the Crows returned to their village. Before entering, all painted their faces black with paint made from water and burned grass, and they impaled the enemy scalps on top of lances or Jim's gun barrel. Then, howling a victory song, they made their appearance. The people greeted them with a wild frenzy of shouts, embraces and stomping. Jim's Indian relatives lavished praise upon him. *Ayee*! Morning Star was truly the bravest of warriors!

Jim soaked up the praise and joined in the victory dance.

All this while he was thinking how best to get the most out of his life with the Indians. The Crow way of life was centered on two activities: raising or stealing horses for profit and warring on enemies. The chief never rallied all the braves for a great battle, as white men did. Any warrior who wished to might lead a raid and often did so because his prestige in the tribe depended on how many *coups* he earned. His friends might or might not join him. So, as Jim slowly learned the language and customs, he did only those things which would enhance his position.

Instead of tearing off whenever some braves

whooped for bloodletting, Jim held off. But when the Blackfeet or Cheyennes threatened the village, Jim roared the loudest, fought the wildest and hardest, and earned many, many *coups*. Luckily he was not killed. In between times he coaxed his relatives into trapping, and his wife and her sisters into preparing the pelts and robes. Once he stopped fretting inwardly about rejoining his white companions, he enjoyed his Indian life to the hilt. After all, what other man in the mountains had it better than he? He had a pretty wife, a comfortable home, plenty of food and excitement, willing helpers, and admiring friends! And as the pile of furs and robes enlarged, he realized that he was also making money.

A year later his Indian father, Big Bowl, told Jim that a large party of Crows would travel two hundred miles to the east in order to trade the villagers' furs at Fort Clarke. This post was built on the upper Missouri River by the American Fur Company.

Jim thrilled at the news because he was anxious to reestablish contact with a fur company. But the Crows would not let him make the trip. He vowed he would not try to escape. He argued he could bargain for better returns with the fur post clerk. But the chief and warrior members of the tribal council refused to let him go.

Jim knew better than to show his disappointment.

He daubed his initials on each of his pelts and robes and figured their worth. He told the chief what he expected in return in trade goods and received most of his requests. His family gloried in his wealth and the generosity he extended to them all.

Now Jim's life settled into a pattern for many more months. In the book which he would dictate to Mr. Bonner years later, over three hundred pages would be devoted to descriptions of the bloody raids and battles he shared with the Crows against their enemies. There is no space to mention them here. But gradually Jim acquired enough *coups* so he was allowed to lead war parties on his own. He was given a new Indian name, which meant Bloody Arm. Still, Jim never took to the war path unless the outcome would benefit him. Partly he wanted the Crows to think that his "medicine," or spirit power, was strong and that he was a valuable asset to the tribe. But also, Jim was first, last, and always a hard-headed business man.

In another year or two Jim was allowed to travel with the Crows to Fort Clarke. He held back while the braves and squaws completed their trading. Neither the chief trader, James Kipp, nor his clerk gave Jim a second glance. After all, he spoke the Crow language and dressed like a Crow. With his dark hair falling down his back and his face plucked free of hair, in Crow fashion, he looked like a Crow.

But Jim couldn't remain unnoticed for long. When one of the braves had a hard time telling Kipp what he wanted, Jim, grinning and with eyes merry, spoke out. "Gentlemen, that Indian wants scarlet cloth."

As Jim said, "If a bomb shell had exploded in the fort, they could not have been more astonished."

Since the Crows could understand very little English, Jim was safe in identifying himself to James Kipp. Jim drove a hard bargain with the trader and demanded far more for his furs than Kipp returned to the Indians. So the Crows were agoggle at the results of Jim's dickering.

Next Jim did something which he had planned carefully beforehand. Kipp never let his Indian customers trade furs for guns, knowing well that many would quickly turn these against white men. So Jim worked hard and earnestly to convince Kipp that he should sell Jim many guns, which he in turn would trade to the Crows for many, many furs. Then Jim would trade these furs to Kipp, enhancing his company's profits. Since the Crows were "friendlies" and Jim vowed to keep them that way, Kipp finally consented. He was so impressed with Jim's trading ability that he promptly hired him at a salary of $800 a year to secure the entire Crow trade for Fort Clarke. Jim accepted the offer with joy. This was a fat bonus he had not anticipated!

When the Crows returned to their village, Jim

spread out the rifles for all to see. He told the chief and warriors that he would teach them to be the best shooters in the West, so the Crows would win many victories. Of course, they must give him many, many furs in exchange. The warriors readily agreed. After all, they didn't have to do the trapping. They made the younger men and women bear the brunt of it. Within months the Crows entered a long period of victories and almost overwhelming self-esteem. It was very much to Jim's credit that he held the warriors to their promise of never turning their guns against white men and their families.

As the years rolled by, Jim was voted a member of the ruling council of the Crow nation and finally was named chief of all the people. By this time he was the wealthiest of all Crows. He had several wives whom he kept busy tanning skins and attending to his comforts. He owned hundreds of fine horses and traded for goods valued at thousands of dollars. Knowing only too well how white men used whisky to cheat and debauch the Indians, Jim refused to allow the Crows to have liquor. If they got hold of some while visiting the fur post, he either punished or humiliated them. If white men tried to sneak into Crow country to peddle the rotgut for valuable furs, Jim ran them off with such threats they never returned. But only on this point could Jim be called a dictator. In all other matters, he encouraged the Crows to continue their Indian way of life. He did not try to change them to the white man's way of life. He respected their *Indianness*.

Fourteen years later Jim told the Crows he must travel to St. Louis to straighten out his business affairs. He promised he would return, though secretly he had decided to leave them forever. The closer he came to St. Louis, the more excited he became. How much more settled the country was! How crowded the city was! Why, there were steamboats plying the Missouri!

After attending to his business at the headquarters of the American Fur Company, Jim discovered that he was now worth over ten thousand dollars. This was a tidy fortune for a white man. For a Negro it was almost unheard of. But some of his joy dimmed when he learned that many of his trapper friends were now dead. And after he sought out his real family, he discovered that his parents were long dead, and his brothers and sisters scattered. Only two sisters remained in St. Louis. But they lived in a poor house, in a poor section of town. Even though they were free people, their lot was as miserable as that of the many Negro slaves in the region. Jim found it almost impossible to accept this change. He had been a free man for so long and had been treated as an equal by his trapper friends. He couldn't accept the fact that in the eyes of the white men in St. Louis, he was a person of absolutely no worth.

But the deepest blow of all was realizing that while his sisters welcomed him, they were obviously wary of this brother who looked and acted like an Indian.

Jim spoke with deep feeling of this moment, which he described to Mr. Bonner as follows. "I thought of my Indian home, and of the unsophisticated hearts I had left behind me. There is not the elegance there, the luxury, the refined breeding, but there is a crude plenty, prairies studded with horses, and room to wander without any man to call your steps in question. My child was there, and his mother, whom I loved. A return there was in no way unnatural. I had acquired their habits, and was in some manner useful to them."

Sadly Jim realized that he had no ties holding him to St. Louis. So he went home, to the Crows.

10

"When the green grass decks the plain..."

While Jim was relaxing in St. Louis, trappers hired by a rival fur outfit visited the Crows. They told them that employees of the American Fur Company who were jealous of Jim's position among the Crows had killed him. They urged them to take revenge by attacking all the fur posts and trappers employed by that company. This included a brand new post, Fort Cass, which at Jim's suggestion was now being built at the confluence of the Bighorn and Little Bighorn rivers, in present Montana.

The Crows became violently excited and drummed up a war dance. Fortunately, wiser heads among the older warriors prevailed. They told the people that they would send messengers to Fort Cass to find out if Jim, whom they now called Medicine Calf, was alive or dead. If he had been

killed they would go on the rampage. So a delega-
tion called on Sam Tulloch, the trader in charge of
Fort Cass. The warriors delivered an ultimatum
which said, in effect, "Give us back our chief or die."

In vain Tulloch tried to convince the grim-faced
Crows that the rival trappers were lying. No white
man would ever kill a man as brave and strong as
Medicine Calf. The Crows sneered and accused
Tulloch of lying to them!

To save his life, the poor fellow sent messengers
with dispatches to Fort Clarke. In these he pleaded
with James Kipp to locate Jim, and get him to hurry
back to the Crows . . . even if the company had to
pay Jim to do so.

The Crows quieted down after the messengers
left. They knew how long it would take a small
party to travel from the Bighorn to St. Louis and
back. They agreed to take no action until they had
some proof that Medicine Calf was alive or dead.
But, they warned, if the chief did not return by the
time the chokecherries were ripe in the fall, they
would launch their attack. To make sure the trader
and his people did not escape, the Crows encircled
the post with their tepees, and kept constant watch
over it.

Within five weeks Kipp's messengers, who were
boatmen, paddled down the Missouri and con-
tacted Jim in St. Louis. He sent them back upriver
at once to tell Kipp and Tulloch and the Crows that

he would indeed return when the chokecherries were ripe. Of course, by this time Jim had already decided to return to Crow country, but he didn't let on. Instead, he appeared indifferent. The fur company officials offered him one thousand dollars to leave at once. Still Jim hedged. The officials were frantic. They had over one hundred thousand dollars worth of furs stored at Fort Cass and Fort Clarke, and over a hundred employees' lives were in danger. So they upped the price to five thousand dollars.

Jim snapped at the offer before the tight-fisted officials had second thoughts about the money. He hired two men to accompany him and left as soon as the needed provisions and gear were assembled and placed on the backs of three mules. Fifty-three days after their departure, they reined up on high ground overlooking Fort Cass. Below was the sparkling Bighorn River, the tiny post, and hundreds of Crow tepees.

Naturally a chief does not ride in, unannounced, to his people. One of Jim's men rode to the village with the good news. The people began to shout and race around wildly. Jim's wives returned with the messenger, bringing the rawhide cases which contained Jim's handsome chief's ceremonial suit and

The three men reined up on high
ground overlooking Fort Cass.

trappings. The buckskin shirt was tanned as soft as velvet and ornamented with bright beads, bits of mirrors, ermine tails, elk teeth, silver bells, and tufts of hair from Blackfeet scalps.

Jim's men watched open-mouthed as this man, whom they considered just another ordinary mountain man, and a mulatto at that, was transformed before their eyes into the heroic figure of a Crow chieftain. When fully attired with the heavy feathered headdress binding his long dark hair, Jim mounted a fine war horse. With the reins in one hand and his war shield in the other, Jim—or rather, Medicine Calf—returned to his people.

The Crows were wild with joy. For two weeks the sound of singing and drumming never quieted.

For many months Jim resumed the Indian way of life. Perhaps, had he never visited St. Louis and glimpsed a more civilized way of life, he might have been content. But now discontent set in. As chief, he had to lead many raids against the Cheyennes and Blackfeet. He had to help drive out the Sioux who had been forced off their Dakota hunting grounds and tried to take over the Crow country.

He expressed his feelings this way. "In good truth, I was tired of savage life under any aspect. I knew that, if I remained with them, it would be war and carnage to the end of the chapter, and my mind sickened at the repetition of such scenes. Savage life admits of no repose to the man who desires to retain the character of a great brave. There is no retiring upon your laurels."

Rather than spend the rest of his life as an Indian warrior Jim again decided to leave the Crows forever. It almost broke his heart to leave his first wife, whom he loved deeply, and their oldest son, whom Jim had named Black Panther. But he was enough of a realist to know that they would be miserable if taken from their homeland and relatives. Worse, they would be badly treated wherever Jim settled in a white community. So for their sake, and his too, he must go alone.

Once more Jim told the people that he was going to St. Louis on business. "I told them to credit no reports of my death, for they would be false. The whites would never kill me." Over and over he promised them that he would return. Therefore, they must not believe lies told them nor turn against the white people. They must be friendly, always.

The Crows promised and prepared a happy send-off for their beloved chief. In the morning, after he had said farewell to all the relatives and friends, he promised his wife and first son, "When the green grass decks the plain, I will return to you."

Then he mounted his horse and rode away, sorrowing, positive he would never see them again.

11

Jim Becomes Famous from Coast to Coast

When Jim reached St. Louis, he learned the United States Army was recruiting soldiers and scouts for a campaign against the Seminole Indians in Florida. Thinking it might be a lark to travel to new country, Jim signed on as a scout. But he had been a chief too long to be content with the life of a lowly private, and he left the army in six months. He disliked the hot climate and flat, featureless land and was terribly homesick for the mountains.

Back in St. Louis again, he joined Bill Sublette and Louis Vasquez in a trading venture. They bought several tons of merchandise, loaded them on wagons, and took off with a strong company to trade with any Indians they might find along the upper reaches of the Platte and Arkansas rivers, in present-day Colorado. Over twenty years had passed since Jim first ventured out across the country. How times had changed! There were settlements far out on the plains now and numerous trading posts and military forts. America truly was moving westward, but no longer on foot or horseback. Now steamboats plied the Missouri River all the way to the mountains, and wagons were rolling over South Pass onto the west slope. The great migration to Oregon was just now getting under way.

Out in Colorado Jim met William Bent whose family operated a large trading post near the headwaters of the Arkansas River. Although many tribes of the Southwest and canyon country such as Comanches, Utes, Apaches, and others traded at Bent's Fort, Bill Bent's closest ties were with the Southern Cheyennes. They were the same nation as those who raided through Crow country, but their activities were centered more in Colorado, western Kansas, and the Arkansas River valley. Because the mountain country was so vast and Indians so numerous, Bill Bent welcomed Jim and his partners. He even told them there was much money to be made trading with the Northern Cheyennes. Not surprisingly, Jim, Sublette, and Vasquez decided to visit the Northern Cheyennes.

Because Bent knew of Jim's long sojourn with the Crows, he took it for granted the partners would split up, and Jim would give the Northern Cheyennes a wide berth. When Jim said calmly that he intended to trade among them, Ben exclaimed, "Beckwourth, don't you know they will kill you if they discover you?"

Jim replied that he thought not. He knew Indians better than any other civilized man in the West. He knew they respected courage and a great warrior's achievements, even when that warrior was an enemy. Also, he knew, or at least hoped he knew, how he could appeal to the Cheyennes' pride so they would not kill him.

Bent, Vasquez, and Sublette pleaded with Jim to stay away from the Cheyennes. But Jim refused. It is to the credit of Jim's partners that they stuck with him every mile of the long haul into the heart of Cheyenne country. They knew full well that if Jim was killed, they would be too.

In time the traders reached a large village. Since none spoke the language, Jim used sign language, which all mountain tribes understood, to ask if there was a Crow captive among them who could interpret for him. When this person, a woman, appeared she recognized Jim as the great Crow chief. She almost fainted with fear.

But Jim told her, "Tell the Cheyennes that I have fought them many winters; that I have killed so many of their people that I am buried with their scalps. I have taken a host of their women and children prisoners. I have ridden their horses until their backs were sore. I have eaten their fat buffalo until I was full. Now I have killed a great Crow chief, and am obliged to run away, or be killed by them. I have come to the Cheyennes, who are the bravest people in the mountains, as I do not wish to be killed by any of the inferior tribes. I have come here to be killed by the Cheyennes, cut up, and thrown out for their dogs to eat, so that they may say they have killed a great Crow chief."

The Crow captive took a long time to say all this and had to repeat the story many times until all the Cheyennes present had heard it. Meanwhile Jim and his friends sat cross-legged on the ground, smoking calmly, and looking very unconcerned.

Old Bark, the chief, and his warriors withdrew to the council lodge to discuss whether this great Crow chief must be killed. They knew his medicine was strong and how much he had done for the Crows. They didn't want that medicine turned against them. Finally they emerged from the lodge. Old Bark spoke loudly so all could hear. "Warrior, we have seen you before. We know you. We know you are a great brave. You say you have killed many of our warriors. We know you do not lie. We like a great brave. We will not kill you. You shall live!"

Jim rose on steady legs, and answered, "If you

will not kill me, I will live with you." He promised to trade fairly with them. He said his arm was strong and would help them against their enemies, that he would not cheat the Cheyennes, nor sell them whisky.

So Jim's faith in his own profound knowledge of Indian character saved the day. After smoking a pipe with Old Bark and the warriors, he and his partners opened their packs and distributed many presents. And from that day on, for many years Jim carried on a thriving trade with the Cheyennes.

However, one thing he could not do. He could not keep the Cheyennes from getting liquor from illicit white peddlers. As they developed an over-powering craze for the rotgut, they deteriorated in every way and often were drunk for days on end. They lost interest in trapping, and soon had no furs to trade.

About this same time the fashion craze for beaver hats came to an end. Now every gentleman and lady had to have a silk hat. The price of beaver skins dropped so drastically in the wholesale fur market at St. Louis that the fur companies no longer accepted the skins in trade. Now they turned to trading in buffalo robes, which were in great demand.

These two changes ruined any future profit in trading with the Cheyennes, so Jim and his partners

12

Return to the Crows

The last paragraph of Jim's book begins: "I now close the chapter of my eventful life. I feel that time is pressing. The reminiscences of the past, stripped of all that was unpleasant, come crowding upon me."

In all fairness it must be pointed out that Jim enjoyed many advantages denied to others of his race and time. He had a loving family, a happy childhood, and a father who saw to it that Jim learned a profitable craft. When Jim entered the fur trade, he associated with men who treated him as an equal and respected him for his courage, ability, and wit. But beyond that, Jim made his own way and created much of what seemed to be good luck. He brought as much or more good to a situation as he personally derived from it. Never once in his book did Jim ask for sympathy or help. Never once did he feel sorry for himself or bemoan the hardships suffered. These were the prices one paid for being a mountain man. Jim Beckwourth paid that price over and over without a whimper and fought on for the exciting free life he determined to have.

Although Jim said that he felt time pressing in on him, he had more good years ahead. By 1859 the great rush to California had ended. As traffic past his door dwindled, Jim could have dawdled away his remaining years on his ranch. But that was not his way. The years of roaming the mountains had left Jim with an incurably itchy foot. So he sold the ranch and boarded a stagecoach bound for Denver, Colorado. But a couple of days of being bounced around on the hard seat and the strangling dust so disgusted him that he quit the newfangled modern way of traveling. He bought a good riding horse, a strong-backed mule, camp gear, and staple foods, and continued on at his own pace.

Denver was booming then, thanks to the many gold discoveries in the surrounding mountains. As Jim strolled the streets jammed with freight wagons and mule trains, he heard someone mention the name Vasquez. Could that be old Lou Vasquez, his one-time partner? Jim asked directions and soon stepped into a large store stocked to the rafters with trade goods. When he asked a black-aproned clerk for old Lou, a young fellow came forward.

Jim squinted at him, and asked if he was old Lou's *pup*.

The young man grinned and said he was Pike Vasquez, old Lou's nephew. When he learned his visitor was Jim Beckwourth, he welcomed him in true mountain man fashion—with a whoop and holler, a bear hug embrace, a bone-crunching hand-clasp, and a glass of choice whisky. Knowing how mountain men love to yarn, Pike invited Jim to step over to the nearest tavern. Then he told him that old Lou and a host of other cronies were now dead. Jim accepted the news calmly.

Before they parted that night, Pike made Jim an offer. Although Jim claimed he had plenty of money and didn't need a job, Pike sensed that the old man was really lonely, though he would never admit it. So he asked Jim to come to work for him in the store. That way Jim could see new faces every day, indulge in the dickering that was second nature to him, and advise the pale-faced greenhorns what to buy and how to keep from getting killed by the Indians roundabout.

Jim was delighted with the offer and accepted it. He appeared for work every morning freshly bar-bered, and clad in a good wool business suit and polished boots. Not long after, possibly at Pike's suggestion, a newspaper reporter for *The Rocky Mountain News*, published in Denver, interviewed Jim and wrote an article about his amazing life. The reporter admitted later that he had expected to see a rough, illiterate backwoodsman. Instead he was "most agreeably surprised to find him a polished gentleman, possessing a fund of general information of which few can boast. He is now sixty-two years of age, but looks scarce fifty, hale, hearty, and straight as an arrow."

In 1864 Jim had had enough of city life. He bought a ranch watered by the sparkling Platte River. Here he had a fine cabin built and settled down to the kind of life he loved. He found a pretty young Indian woman to take over the household chores. He would have nothing to do with planting crops or putting cattle to graze on the wild grass which had once fed elk and buffalo. Instead Jim bought a few head of sturdy Indian ponies and turned them loose to graze in the old way. In good weather Jim trapped beaver for Pike Vasquez to sell in his Denver store. Greenhorns and tourists paid a good price for beaver skins. On winter nights Jim lounged by his fire and dreamed of the old days. In his mind he talked again with General Ashley, and Tom Fitzpatrick, and a host of others. He relived the raids, and rendezvous, and the years with the Crows. The Crows . . . Was the beautiful Indian girl who had been his favorite wife still alive? Had his first son, Black Panther, grown strong and replaced his father as chief of the Crow nation?

When Jim's mind cleared, he would tell himself that he probably never would know the answers to those questions. True, he had promised the Crows, "When the green grass decks the plains, I will return to you." Well, that was one promise he would never fulfill, even if he had a mind to. The years were long gone when his legs would carry him up canyons and over the mountains to Crow country.

In 1862 a small party of prospectors made a fabulously rich gold strike in the mountains bordering on the western edge of the Crow country, in present Montana. As the exciting news trickled back along the trails, wagon trains and freight wagons bound for the Pacific Northwest peeled off the well-known routes and blazed a short cut to the Montana diggings. This new route cut diagonally across Crow country. The Crows tried to turn back the wagons. The whites answered with bullets. The Crows returned the fire and unleashed all their fury on the unfortunate families.

The few who escaped appealed to the federal government to send a company of soldiers to protect the wagon trains as they angled across Crow country. When a small contingent of soldiers marched out from a fort in northern Wyoming to clear the way, the Crows tore them to bits.

Army officials and government leaders pondered how best to handle the problem without mounting a full-scale campaign against the entire Crow nation. During the talks, someone remembered that Jim Beckwourth had once been a chief of the Crows and had been successful in keeping them friendly toward white people. Could he help, they wondered.

More important, would he help?

Jim would. He readily agreed to return to the Crow country, if the Army furnished him an escort and a pack train loaded with gifts. If he appeared with anything less, the Crows would not think he was a great chief. They would think he no longer had strong medicine, or spirit power. The Army officers let Jim have his way.

Jim's homecoming to Crow country was all that he could have hoped for or his Indian people could have wanted. His favorite wife was still alive and wept for joy. His son, Black Panther, was now chief of the nation. Many of the old people remembered him. The younger ones treated him with great respect.

After a welcoming feast and distribution of the gifts, Jim called Black Panther and the warrior council to meet with him and the white chiefs who had accompanied him. He asked the Crows why they had turned against his white brothers. They replied that white hunters had killed off all the buffalo so the people were hungry; that the young men and women were addicted to the whisky brought in by white peddlers; that some white families had fenced off land along their favorite rivers and refused to let the Indians camp there, or gather berries, or fish and hunt. Soon, they said, with tears streaming down their cheeks, they would have no place to go and nothing to eat.

Jim described these complaints to the government officials. He told them that the only way to keep the Crows at peace was to set aside thousands of acres surrounding the Bighorn River for their exclusive use, so the Crows could carry on their way of life without interference from white settlers. The officials agreed. After much dickering and many speeches, Jim got the Crows to accept the terms of a peace treaty. The chief and warriors daubed their fingers in paint, and placed their marks on the parchment on which the terms were written. Since Jim still could not write, he followed suit.

As the council drew to a close, Jim announced that much as he wanted to stay with the Crows, he must go away again.

At first the Crows were too stunned to speak. But soon they began pleading with him to stay. They reminded him that when he was with them, times were good, and victories many because his medicine was strong. After he had gone away the second time, the people had fallen on evil times. Now that he was back, he must stay so his medicine would bring back the former glorious days. In their eyes, Jim's medicine was still strong. How else could he have come back escorted by soldiers and other white chiefs and distributed so many gifts?

But Jim steadfastly refused their pleas. He was sorry but he must leave. The Crows hung their heads. Some wept, some wailed, some withdrew to their lodges so they would not have to see Medicine Calf turn his back on his people forever.

Feeling that he had accomplished all he could, Jim suggested that the officials and soldiers get ready to depart. But before the packing was completed, a number of warriors addressed him. They said the people wished to honor him with a feast and dance, as in the old days. His wives would prepare his favorite dishes. His relatives would sing his favorite songs. The people would dance all night in homage to Medicine Calf.

Jim was deeply touched. He knew a few more hours delay would not matter. Actually, it might be better to let the Crows say goodby in their fashion.

A great bonfire was lighted. The white men were escorted to places of honor in a circle around it and seated on the best buffalo robes. Jim had the place of

Jim had been poisoned.

honor next to his son, the chief. His favorite wife served him a thick spicy meat stew. All the Crow guests seemed very happy. They laughed and sang. Even the white men relaxed and enjoyed themselves.

But suddenly Jim cried out in pain. Seconds later he was dead.

Obviously, Jim had been poisoned.

When the white men recovered from shock, they asked through an interpreter if Jim had been poisoned.

The Crows freely acknowledged the crime. Their excuse was that since a great chief's medicine remained strong forever, it mattered not at all whether he was alive or dead, as long as he was with his people. "He has been our good medicine," they said. This is why they had plotted to keep him with them, always.

The interpreter then asked the white men to leave. He said the Crows wanted to start their long period of mourning. They would bury their chief with all the honors a tribe could bestow on this man whom they loved so deeply that they could not bear to part with him. And after the prayers and incantations and dancing, they would bury him under the green-grassed plain so his spirit need never leave Crow country.

So Jim returned to the Crows after all and, as he wished, never left the mountains.

Selected Bibliography

BONNER, T. D. *The Life and Adventures of James P. Beckwourth*, edited, with an introduction by Bernard De Voto. New York: Alfred A. Knopf, 1931.

CHITTENDEN, HIRAM MARTIN. *The American Fur Trade of the Far West*. New York: F. P. Harper, 1902.

DE VOTO, BERNARD. *Across the Wide Missouri*. Boston: Houghton, Mifflin Company, 1947.

HAFEN, LEROY R. *"The last years of James P. Beckwourth." The Colorado Magazine*, August, 1928.

LAVENDER, DAVID. *Bent's Fort*. Garden City, N.Y.: Doubleday & Company, 1954.

MUMEY, NOLIE. *James Pierson Beckwourth, 1856–1866*. Denver: Fred A. Rosenstock, The Old West Publishing Company, 1957.

Index